Literary Passages:
Close Reading

Marcia Miller & Martin Lee

NEW YORK • TORONTO • LONDON • AUCKLAND • SYDNEY
MEXICO CITY • NEW DELHI • HONG KONG • BUENOS AIRES

Cover design: Tannaz Fassihi
Cover illustration: Patrick George
Interior design: Kathy Massaro
Interior illustrations by Bari Weissman, except page 22 by James Graham Hale

"Never Mind, March" © 1983 by Scholastic Inc. Used by permission.

ISBN: 978-0-545-79384-1
Copyright © 2016 by Scholastic Inc.
All rights reserved.
Printed in the U.S.A.
Published by Scholastic Inc.

2 3 4 5 6 7 8 9 10   40   23 22 21 20 19 18 17 16

Contents

Introduction 5

Teaching Routine for Close Reading and Purposeful Text Marking 7

Connections to the Standards 9

Comprehension Skill Summary Cards 10

Literary Text Passages

Character

1. Coach Sam (270 L)................................ Sports Story 14

2. Kitchen Brothers (310 L)..................... Cooking Story 16

3. Getting Across (380 L) .... Folktale 18

Setting

4. The Legend of Swampy Pond (360 L)............ Legend 20

5. Never Mind, March (N/A) .... Poem 22

6. To the Moon! (410 L)... Science Fiction 24

Key Events & Details

7. A Surprise Trip (200 L) .... Travel Story 26

8. Rolling, Rolling, Rolling... (280 L) .... Sports Story 28

9. Go Fly a Kite! (380 L).. Springtime Story 30

10. In the Attic (410 L) .... Mystery 32

Sequence of Events

11. A Silly Dream (270 L)................................ Fantasy 34

12. Treasure Hunt (350 L) .... Birthday Story 36

13. Painting Puff (370 L) .... Art Story 38

Problem & Solution

14. The Tired Clock (210 L) .... Fantasy 40

15. Pip Solves a Problem (300 L) .... Adventure 42

16. Puppy School (360 L) .... Dog Story...44

Compare & Contrast

17. Two Small Pets (250 L)............................. Pet Story..46

18. Safe Trails (290 L)................................... Nature Story 48

19. Fox and Cat (300 L) .... Fable 50

20. Cartoon Characters (370 L) .... Descriptions..52

Answer Key 54

Introduction

Reading, discussing, and sharing literary texts contributes greatly to the development of well-rounded minds. Exposure to diverse literary forms, characters, and plots, set in varied time periods and cultures, models for readers how the world works. Literary texts help us learn how people explore, interact, struggle, grow, and solve problems. In short, reading fiction enriches us.

Modern science supports that the human brain is hard-wired for stories. All cultures immerse their children in stories that explain the ways of the world while engaging their emotions. Although many students enjoy reading fiction, navigating the wide variety of literary texts poses challenges for evolving readers. Students may lack sufficient vocabulary or background knowledge to follow along, and some genres may be unfamiliar to them at first. This is why exposing students more frequently to rich literary texts and introducing them to active reading-comprehension strategies are now key components of successful reading instruction. Useful strategies, clearly taught, can empower readers to approach literary texts purposefully, closely, and independently. Such active tools provide students with a foundation for success not only in school, but for the rest of their lives.

> **Connections to the Standards**
>
> The chart on page 9 details how the lessons in this book will help your students meet the more rigorous demands of today's reading standards for literature.

Text Marking: A Powerful Active-Reading Strategy

To improve their comprehension of literary texts, students must actively engage with the material. Careful and consistent text marking by hand is one valuable way to accomplish this. To begin with, by numbering paragraphs, students can readily identify the location of useful narrative details when discussing a piece. By circling main characters, underlining pertinent clues to setting or sequence, and boxing key vocabulary, students interact directly with the text, making it more digestible in the process. But the true goal of teaching text marking is to help students internalize an effective close-reading strategy, not to have them show how many marks they can make on a page.

Purposeful text marking intensifies a reader's focus. It helps readers identify narrative elements as they read, and recognize and isolate key details or connect relevant ideas presented in the text. For instance, boxing words like *first, then, next,* and *finally* can clarify the sequence of ideas or events in a passage. By circling expressions like *the trouble is* or *one answer is,* students learn to identify problems and their solutions. When students are asked to compare and contrast elements in a passage, boxing signal words, such as *both, but,* or *however,* can make identifying similarities and differences more apparent. Furthermore, the physical act of writing by hand, in itself, helps students not only process what they read, but remember it as well.

About the Passages

The 20 reproducible passages in this book, which vary in genres, topics, purposes, tones, and tasks, address six key reading-comprehension skills, from identifying character, settings, and key events and details, to sequencing and finding problem-solution relationships. Consult the table of contents to see the scope of skills, genres, topics, and Lexile scores of the passages. (The poem on page 22 does not include a Lexile score because poetry is excluded from Lexile measurements.) The Lexile scores fall within the ranges recommended for first graders. (The scores for grade 1, revised to reflect the more rigorous demands of today's higher standards, range from 190 to 420. This range addresses the variety commonly seen in typical first grade classrooms.)

Each passage appears on its own page, beginning with the title, the genre or topic, and the main comprehension skill the passage addresses. The passages include illustrations as visual elements, as well as typical text elements, such as words in capital letters and boldface type.

The passages are organized to help scaffold young students' understanding of each comprehension skill. For example, in the first passage of the compare and contrast section, students identify one way two pets are alike and a target signal word. The second passage has them identify one way two settings differ and a key signal word. The next passage has them identify one way the characters are alike and one way they are different, and locate two signal words. In the last passage, students identify two ways the characters are alike and different, and recognize four pertinent signal words.

Until your students are reading independently, the passages will work best as shared reading activities using an interactive whiteboard or document camera, or during guided reading so that you can scaffold and support readers. (See the next page for a close-reading routine to model for students.)

Reading-Comprehension Question Pages

Following each passage is a reproducible "Do More" page of text-dependent comprehension questions: two are multiple-choice questions that call for a single response and a brief, text-based explanation to justify that choice. The other is an open-response item. The questions address a range of comprehension strategies and skills. All questions share the goal of ensuring that students engage in close reading of the text, grasp its key ideas, and provide text-based evidence to support their answers. Keep additional paper on hand so students have ample space to write complete and thorough answers.

An answer key (pages 54–63) includes annotated versions of each marked passage and sample answers to its related questions. Maintain flexibility in assessing student responses, as some markings and answers to open-response questions may vary. (Since students are likely to mark different places in the text for particular skills, the annotated versions in the answer key highlight a variety of possible responses.) Encourage students to self-assess and revise their answers as you review the text markings together. This approach encourages discussion, comparison, extension, reinforcement, and correlation to other reading skills.

Teaching Routine for Close Reading and Purposeful Text Marking

Any text can become more accessible to readers once they have learned to bring various strategies, such as purposeful text marking, to the reading process. Here is one suggested routine that may be effective in your classroom.

Preview

- **Engage prior knowledge** of the topic of the passage and its genre. Help students link it to similar topics or examples of the genre they may have read.

- **Identify the reading skill** for which students will be marking the text. Display or distribute the Comprehension Skill Summary Card that applies to the passage. Go over its key ideas. (See Comprehension Skill Summary Cards, page 8, for more.)

Model *(for the first passage, to familiarize students with the process)*

- **Display the passage,** using an interactive whiteboard, document camera, or other resource, and provide students with their own copy. Preview the text with students by having them read the title and look at the illustration.

- **Draw attention to the markings** students will use to enhance their understanding of the passage. Link the text marking box to the Comprehension Skill Summary Card for clarification.

- **Read aloud the passage** as students follow along. Guide students to think about the featured skill and to note any questions they may have on sticky-notes.

- **Mark the text together.** Begin by numbering the paragraphs. Then discuss the choices you make when marking the text, demonstrating and explaining how various text elements support the skill. Check that students understand how to mark the text using the icons and graphics shown in the text marking box.

Read

- **Display each passage for a shared reading experience.** Do a quick-read of the passage together to familiarize students with it. Then read it together a second time, pausing as necessary to answer questions, draw connections, or clarify words. Then read the passage once more, this time with an eye to the features described in the text marking box.

- **Invite students to offer ideas for additional markings.** These might include noting unfamiliar vocabulary, an idiom or phrase they may not understand, or an especially interesting, unusual, or important detail they want to remember. Model how to use sticky-notes, colored pencils, highlighters, question marks, or check marks.

Respond

- **If students are able, have them read the passage independently.** This reading is intended to allow students to mark the text themselves, with your support, as needed. It will also prepare them to discuss the passage and offer their views about it.

- **Have students answer the questions** on the companion Do More page. Depending on the abilities of your students, you might read aloud the questions, and then have them answer orally. Model how to look back at the text markings and other text evidence for assistance. This will help students provide complete and supported responses.

Comprehension Skill Summary Cards

To help students review the six reading-comprehension skills this book addresses and the specific terms associated with each, have them use the reproducible Comprehension Skill Summary Cards (pages 10–12). The boldface terms on each card are the same ones students will identify as they mark the text.

You might duplicate, cut out, and distribute a particular Comprehension Skill Summary Card before assigning a passage that focuses on that skill. Discuss the elements of the skill together to ensure that students fully grasp it. Encourage students to save and collect the cards, which they can use as a set of reading aids to refer to whenever they read any type of literary text. Or display the cards in a reading center in your classroom, where they will be available at all times.

Tips and Suggestions

- The text-marking process is versatile and adaptable. While numbering, boxing, circling, and underlining are the most common methods, you can personalize the strategy for your class if it helps augment the process. You might have students use letters to mark text; they can, for example, write KE to indicate a key event, D to mark a detail, or P for problem and S for solution. Whichever technique you use, focus on the need for consistency of marking.

- You may wish to extend the text-marking strategy by having students identify other aspects of writing, such as confusing words, expressions, or idioms.

Comprehension Skill

Character

Every story tells about someone. A story can have one, two, or more **characters**.

- A **character** is WHO the story is about.
  A character can be a person, an animal, or a thing.

- Read for details that tell about each **character**.

- Read for details that tell about different **characters** so you can tell them apart.

Comprehension Skill

Setting

The **setting** of a story tells <u>where</u> and <u>when</u> the story takes place.

- Read for details that tell <u>where</u> a story takes place.

  It can be a **real** place.

  It can be a **make-believe** place.

- Read for details that tell <u>when</u> the story takes place.

  It might be set in the **present** (now).

  It might be set in the **past** (long ago)

  It might be set in the **future** (years from now).

Comprehension Skill

Compare & Contrast

Authors may tell how people, places, things, or ideas are **alike**. Authors may also tell how they are **different**.

- To **compare** means to tell how things are the same or alike.

- To **contrast** means to tell how things are different.

- **Signal words** give clues that help you compare and contrast.

  Examples for comparing: **both, too, like**, and **also**.

  Examples for contrasting: **but, only, unlike**, and **different**.

Connections to the Standards

The lessons in this book support the College and Career Readiness Anchor Standards for Reading for students in grades K–12. These broad standards, which serve as the basis of many state standards, were developed to establish rigorous educational expectations with the goal of providing students nationwide with a quality education that prepares them for college and careers. The chart below details how the lessons align with specific reading standards for literary text for students in grade 1.

These materials also address language standards, including skills in the conventions of standard English, knowledge of language, and vocabulary acquisition and use. In addition, students meet writing standards as they answer questions about the passages, demonstrating their ability to convey ideas coherently, clearly, and with support from the text.

Reading Standards for Literature	Passages
Key Ideas and Details	
Ask and answer such questions about key details in a text.	1–20
Retell stories, including key details, and demonstrate understanding of their central message or lesson.	1–20
Describe characters, settings, and major events in a story, using key details.	1–20
Craft and Structure	
Identify words and phrases in stories or poems that suggest feelings or appeal to the senses.	2–7, 9–12, 14–16, 18–20
Identify who is telling the story at various points in a text.	3, 7, 11, 13, 14
Integration of Knowledge and Ideas	
Use illustrations and details in a story to describe its characters, setting, or events.	1–20
Compare and contrast the adventures and experiences of characters in stories.	2, 3, 7, 9, 14–17, 19, 20
Range of Reading and Level of Text Complexity	
With prompting and support, read prose and poetry of appropriate complexity for grade 1.	1–20

Source: © Copyright 2010 National Governors Association Center for Best Practices and Council of Chief State School Officers. All rights reserved.

Setting

The **setting** of a story tells <u>where</u> and <u>when</u> the story takes place.

- Read for details that tell <u>where</u> a story takes place.

  It can be a **real** place.

  It can be a **make-believe** place.

- Read for details that tell <u>when</u> the story takes place.

  It might be set in the **present** (now).

  It might be set in the **past** (long ago)

  It might be set in the **future** (years from now).

Character

Every story tells about someone. A story can have one, two, or more **characters.**

- A **character** is WHO the story is about.

  A character can be a person, an animal, or a thing.

- Read for details that tell about each **character.**

- Read for details that tell about different **characters** so you can tell them apart.

Literary Passages: Close Reading (Grade 1)
© 2016 Scholastic Inc.

Sequence of Events

When you read, look for the **order** in which things happen.

- **Events** are actions or things that happen.

- The **sequence** is the order of the events.

- **Signal words** give clues about the sequence of events.

Examples: **first, second, next, then, now, later, after, finally,** and **last.**

Key Events and Details

Things happen in every story. These are **events.**

Events move the story along. Some events are more important than others.

- A **key event** answers the question, "What is an important thing that happens?"

- **Details** tell more about a key event.

Literary Passages: Close Reading (Grade 1)
© 2016 Scholastic Inc.

Compare & Contrast

Authors may tell how people, places, things, or ideas are **alike**. Authors may also tell how they are **different**.

- To **compare** means to tell how things are the same or alike.

- To **contrast** means to tell how things are different.

- **Signal words** give clues that help you compare and contrast.

Examples for comparing: **both, too, like,** and **also**.

Examples for contrasting: **but, only, unlike,** and **different**.

Problem & Solution

Sometimes you will read about **problems** and how they get **solved**.

- A **problem** is a kind of trouble or puzzle.
  A problem needs to be fixed or solved.

- A **solution** is how to solve a problem.
  A solution makes things better.

- **Signal words** give clues to a problem and its solutions.

Examples for problems: **question, need,** and **trouble**.

Examples for solutions: **answer, fix, idea, plan, result,** and **solve**.

Literary Passages: Close Reading (Grade 1)
© 2016 Scholastic Inc.

Literary
Text Passages

Coach Sam

Read the sports story.
Then follow the directions in the box.

Sam has played soccer

since he was four.

He knows the game well.

Now Sam is 44.

He coaches a soccer team.

All the players are in first grade.

Sam helps them kick better.

He shows them how to stop a ball

with their feet.

Sam is a good coach.

He makes soccer fun.

Text Marking

Think about the story.

◯　Circle WHO the story
　　is about.

_____　Underline one detail
　　　about that person.

Literary Passages: Close Reading (Grade 1)
© 2016 Scholastic Inc.

Name _____ Date _____

Coach Sam

▶ **Answer each question. Use the story and picture.**

1 What is TRUE about Sam in this story?

○ A. Sam is tall.

○ B. Sam is in first grade.

○ C. Sam coaches a soccer team.

What helped you answer? _____

_____

_____

2 What makes Sam a good coach?

○ A. He knows the game well.

○ B. He is 44 years old.

○ C. He is funny.

What helped you answer? _____

_____

_____

3 Why does Sam know so much about soccer? Explain.

_____

_____

_____

_____

_____

Literary Passages: Close Reading (Grade 1)
© 2016 Scholastic Inc.

Name _____ Date _____

Kitchen Brothers

Read the cooking story.

Then follow the directions in the box.

Juan and Rico are brothers.

Both are good cooks.

Juan bakes breads.

He works the dough.

He knows just when it is ready.

He makes each bread into a shape.

His best is star bread with nuts.

Rico makes soups and stews.

He loves mixing flavors.

His best dish is lamb and rice stew.

He tastes as he cooks.

It is just right! YUM!

Text Marking

Think about WHO is in this story.

⬭ Circle the name of each character.

___ Underline one detail about each character.

Literary Passages: Close Reading (Grade 1)
© 2016 Scholastic Inc.

Kitchen Brothers

▶ **Answer each question. Use the story and picture.**

1 What is TRUE about Juan and Rico?

    ○ A. They are brothers.

    ○ B. Both bake breads.

    ○ C. Both cook soups and stews.

What helped you answer? _____

_____

_____

2 Which meal might Juan and Rico cook together?

    ○ A. spaghetti and meatballs

    ○ B. bacon and eggs

    ○ C. chicken soup and rye bread

What helped you answer? _____

_____

_____

3 Look at the two brothers. Which is Juan? How do you know?

_____

_____

_____

_____

Literary Passages: Close Reading (Grade 1)
© 2016 Scholastic Inc.

Name _____ Date _____

Getting Across

Read the folktale.

Then follow the directions in the box.

A hungry goat spotted a green field

that looked tasty. But it was across a river.

She stepped onto a wooden bridge.

"STOP!" yelled the mean **troll**

who lived below it. "You cannot cross MY bridge!"

"Please, I am hungry," said the goat politely.

"I only want to get to that green field."

"NO!" roared the angry troll.

"Okay, then, I will swim across."

And she bravely did just that.

troll:
a make-believe
creature that
causes trouble

Text Marking

Think about WHO is in this story.

⬭ Circle each character.

_____ Underline two details

about each character.

Literary Passages: Close Reading (Grade 1)
© 2016 Scholastic Inc.

Getting Across

▶ **Answer each question. Use the folktale and picture.**

1 Why did the goat want to cross the bridge?

    ○ A. She was lost.

    ○ B. She was hungry.

    ○ C. She did not know how to swim.

What helped you answer? _____

_____

_____

2 Where did the troll live?

    ○ A. in a cave   ○ B. on a farm   ○ C. under the bridge

What helped you answer? _____

_____

_____

_____

3 Make a guess. Why didn't the goat just swim across the river in the first place?

_____

_____

_____

_____

Literary Passages: Close Reading (Grade 1)
© 2016 Scholastic Inc.

The Legend of Swampy Pond

Read the legend.

Then follow the directions in the box.

Do you know about Swampy Pond?

The pond looks dark and deep.

The water feels cool.

On a hot summer day, it might seem

just right for a swim.

But old folks tell scary stories about it.

They say a giant catfish lives in that pond.

Nobody has ever seen it.

Nobody wants to.

Text Marking
Think about the legend.
◯   Circle WHERE the legend takes place.
_____   Underline one detail about this place.

Literary Passages: Close Reading (Grade 1)
© 2016 Scholastic Inc.

Name _____ Date _____

The Legend of Swampy Pond

▶ **Answer each question. Use the legend and picture.**

1 People do not swim in Swampy Pond because they think _____.

○ A. the pond is too deep

○ B. a scary catfish lives in it

○ C. the water is not warm enough

What helped you answer? _____

_____

2 Which is TRUE about Swampy Pond?

○ A. It looks dark and deep.

○ B. It is shaped like a giant catfish.

○ C. It looks very scary.

What helped you answer? _____

_____

3 Look at the picture. How do you think the catfish got its name?

_____

_____

_____

_____

Name _____ Date _____

Never Mind, March

Read the poem.

Then follow the directions in the box.

Never mind, March,

We know

When you blow

You're not really mad

Or angry or bad;

You're only blowing the winter away

To get the world ready for April and May.

★ Text Marking ★

Think about the poem.

☐ Draw a box around WHEN the poem takes place.

___ Underline one detail that helps you know.

Literary Passages: Close Reading (Grade 1)

Never Mind, March

▶ **Answer each question. Use the poem and picture.**

1 What season does the poem describe?

○ A. summer   ○ B. autumn   ○ C. spring

What helped you answer? _____

_____

_____

_____

2 What is the weather like in this poem?

○ A. hot   ○ B. windy   ○ C. snowy

What helped you answer? _____

_____

_____

_____

3 Look at the picture. How does it go with the poem?

_____

_____

_____

_____

_____

_____

_____

Name _____ Date _____

To the Moon!

Read the science fiction story.
Then follow the directions in the box.

It is far in the future. The year is 2090.

Rocket ship Luna is speeding

through outer space to the moon.

It carries three guests and two crew members.

Planet Earth looks very small and far away.

Outside the ship, it is totally quiet.

It is dark except for some sparkling stars.

Inside the ship, the crew is busy at work.

They float around with their tools.

The guests stare out Luna's window.

They are excited and jumpy.

They will soon land on the moon!

Text Marking

Think about the science fiction story.

☐ Draw a box around WHEN it takes place.

◯ Circle WHERE it takes place.

✓ Check one detail about WHEN.

_____ Underline one detail about WHERE.

Literary Passages: Close Reading (Grade 1)
© 2016 Scholastic Inc.

Name _____ Date _____

To the Moon!

▶ **Answer each question. Use the science fiction story and picture.**

1 When does the story take place?

○ A. now   ○ B. long, long ago   ○ C. a long time into the future

What helped you answer? _____

_____

_____

2 Which is TRUE about outer space?

○ A. It is quiet and mostly dark.

○ B. It is noisy and bright.

○ C. It is exciting and upside down.

What helped you answer? _____

_____

_____

3 Make a guess. What do you think will happen next in the story?

_____

_____

_____

_____

_____

A Surprise Trip

Read the travel story.

Then follow the directions in the box.

Aunt Ann had a surprise for Rex.

They got into her car.

"Where are we going?" asked Rex.

"You will see," said Aunt Ann.

They drove for 20 minutes and then parked.

"We are at the airport!" cried Rex.

Aunt Ann smiled and took him by the hand.

They walked into a big building.

They rode an elevator to the roof.

There they watched jets land and take off.

"What loud fun!" shouted Rex.

Aunt Ann and Rex hugged.

Text Marking

Think about the story.

◯ Circle two key events that happen.

A Surprise Trip

▶ **Answer each question. Use the story and picture.**

1 What surprise did Aunt Ann have for Rex?

○ A. She bought him a car.

○ B. She took him to the airport.

○ C. She took him to ride an elevator.

What helped you answer? _____

_____

_____

2 Why did Rex say the fun was loud?

○ A. There were crowds of noisy people.

○ B. Loud music was playing.

○ C. Jets make a lot of noise.

What helped you answer? _____

_____

_____

3 Why did Aunt Ann smile at Rex?

_____

_____

_____

_____

_____

Rolling, Rolling, Rolling...

Read the sports story.

Then follow the directions in the box.

Meg went to a bowling party.

She could **barely** lift the heavy ball.

But she did.

Meg put the ball on the line and pushed.

It rolled slowly, very, very slowly.

It rolled slowly, but it kept on going.

It looked like it would not hit

the bowling pins. But it did.

One pin slowly fell, then another, then all the rest.

Everybody cheered.

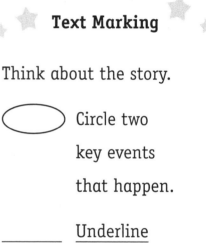

Text Marking

Think about the story.

Circle two key events that happen.

_____ Underline one detail about each event.

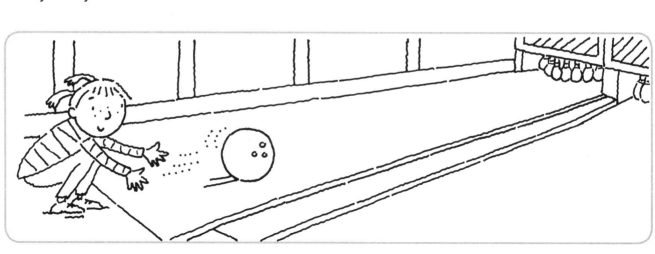

Name _____ Date _____

Rolling, Rolling, Rolling . . .

▶ **Answer each question. Use the story and picture.**

1 Which word means the same as **barely**?

○ A. heavy   ○ B. slowly   ○ C. hardly

What helped you answer? _____

_____

_____

2 What finally happened to Meg's bowling ball?

○ A. It knocked down all the pins.

○ B. It bounced off the pins.

○ C. It stopped rolling.

What helped you answer? _____

_____

_____

3 Look at the picture. How does it help you understand the story?

_____

_____

_____

_____

_____

_____

Literary Passages: Close Reading (Grade 1)

Name _____ Date _____

Go Fly a Kite!

Read the springtime story.
Then follow the directions in the box.

Ko went to the park to fly his kite.

Many people had the same idea

on that windy spring day.

Soon Ko's kite was high in the sky.

Suddenly, his kite got tangled

with another one.

They came crashing down together.

Ko raced to his kite.

A girl raced to her kite.

But when they got there,

both children smiled.

Ko's kite looked like a butterfly.

And so did hers.

Text Marking

Think about the story.

◯ Circle two key events that happen.

_____ Underline one detail about each event.

Literary Passages: Close Reading (Grade 1)
© 2016 Scholastic Inc.

Name _____   Date _____

Go Fly a Kite!

▶ **Answer each question. Use the story and picture.**

1 Why did many people fly kites that day?

　○ A. It was a sunny day.

　○ B. It was a windy day.

　○ C. It was a Saturday.

What helped you answer? _____

_____

_____

2 How did Ko and the girl meet?

　○ A. Their kites got tangled together.

　○ B. They were on the same soccer team.

　○ C. Both children liked animals.

What helped you answer? _____

_____

_____

3 Think about the kites. What made the children smile?

_____

_____

_____

_____

_____

Literary Passages: Close Reading (Grade 1)
© 2016 Scholastic Inc.

In the Attic

Read the mystery story.
Then follow the directions in the box.

Taye climbed to the dusty attic,

which was full of old boxes and junk.

He opened a wooden trunk.

Inside he found a furry wolf mask.

Taye put it on and acted wild.

Suddenly, he howled in surprise.

Another wolf was in the attic,

staring at him!

Taye raced downstairs to his room

and shut the door.

When he looked in his mirror,

he smiled. What did he see?

Text Marking

Think about the story.

◯ Circle two key events that happen.

_____ Underline two details about each event.

Name _____ Date _____

In the Attic

▶ **Answer each question. Use the story and picture.**

1 What did Taye find in the wooden trunk?

○ A. some junk   ○ B. a mirror   ○ C. a mask

What helped you answer? _____

_____

_____

2 Why did Taye race downstairs to his room?

○ A. He got scared.   ○ B. The phone rang.   ○ C. He was being wild.

What helped you answer? _____

_____

_____

3 Think about the mystery. What made Taye smile when he looked in his mirror?

_____

_____

_____

_____

_____

_____

_____

Literary Passages: Close Reading (Grade 1)
© 2016 Scholastic Inc.

A Silly Dream

Read the fantasy story.
Then follow the directions in the box.

Gina was flying through the air.

The sky was pink.

It was the color of bubble gum.

The trees below were blue and gold.

Big balloons covered the ground.

Gina wanted a closer look.

First, she tapped each balloon with her toe.

Each turned into a singing duck.

Then, she fed them bread from her pocket.

"Wake up, Gina!

Time to get ready for school," called Dad.

Text Marking

Find the sequence of events in the dream.

☐ Draw boxes around the signal words **first** and **then**.

___ Underline two events.

1-2 Number the events in order.

A Silly Dream

▶ **Answer each question. Use the story and picture.**

1 What had the color of bubble gum?

○ A. the sky ○ B. the trees ○ C. the balloons

What helped you answer? _____

_____

_____

2 What happened after Gina tapped each balloon?

○ A. She tapped her toes.

○ B. She woke up from her dream.

○ C. It turned into a singing duck.

What helped you answer? _____

_____

_____

3 How can you tell that Gina was dreaming? Give two reasons.

_____

_____

_____

_____

_____

_____

Literary Passages: Close Reading (Grade 1)
© 2016 Scholastic Inc.

Treasure Hunt

Read the birthday story.
Then follow the directions in the box.

It was Nick's birthday.

He was going on a treasure hunt.

He had a list of what to look for.

Things were hidden all over his home.

First, he found the kazoo.

It was hiding inside Mom's fuzzy slipper.

Next, he found the comic book.

It was tucked under the green pillow.

Then, he found the set of star stickers.

They were behind the big salad bowl.

Nick had five more birthday treasures

to find. Where might they be?

Text Marking

Mark the sequence
of treasures Nick found.

☐ Draw boxes around
the signal words
first, **next**,
and **then**.

_____ Underline three
things Nick found.

1-2-3 Number the treasures
in order.

Name _____ Date _____

Treasure Hunt

▶ **Answer each question. Use the story and picture.**

1 What was the second thing Nick found?

○ A. the list   ○ B. the kazoo   ○ C. the comic book

What helped you answer? _____

_____

_____

2 Where did Nick find the kazoo?

○ A. under the green pillow

○ B. in Mom's fuzzy slipper

○ C. behind the big salad bowl

What helped you answer? _____

_____

_____

3 Make a guess. What do you think Nick will do next?

_____

_____

_____

_____

_____

_____

Literary Passages: Close Reading (Grade 1)
© 2016 Scholastic Inc.

Painting Puff

Read the art story.
Then follow the directions in the box.

I like to paint.

I really like to paint animals.

I will paint a picture of Granny's cat for her.

First, I will look through photos of Puff

to pick one I like.

Then, I will get my pencils to sketch Puff.

The photo will help me.

After that, I will get my watercolor paints

and brush.

Painting the picture will be fun.

Last, I will sign my name, Max.

⭐ Text Marking ⭐

Mark the sequence of events for painting Puff.

☐	Draw boxes around the signal words **first, then, after that**, and **last**.
_____	Underline four events.
1-2-3-4	Number the events in order.

Name _____ Date _____

Painting Puff

▶ **Answer each question. Use the story and picture.**

1 Who is telling the story?

○ A. Max   ○ B. Granny   ○ C. Puff

What helped you answer? _____

_____

_____

2 What does the painter do after choosing a photo?

○ A. The painter gets out watercolor paints.

○ B. The painter makes a pencil sketch.

○ C. The painter makes a picture frame.

What helped you answer? _____

_____

_____

3 Make a guess. Why does the painter use a photo to help paint Puff?

_____

_____

_____

_____

_____

_____

_____

Literary Passages: Close Reading (Grade 1)
© 2016 Scholastic Inc.

Name _____ Date _____

The Tired Clock

Read the fantasy story.
Then follow the directions in the box.

"Hey, Sara, look over here!"

The alarm clock was talking.

Sara heard the small voice.

"I have a problem," said the clock.

"I feel slow and tired. Can you help me?"

Sara had the perfect solution.

She went to the kitchen for new batteries.

Next, she opened the clock.

Then, she took out the old batteries

and put in new ones.

"Tick-tock! You fixed me! Thank you,"

said the clock.

"You are very welcome," said Sara.

★ Text Marking

Find the problem and
the solution.

[ ] Draw boxes around
the signal words
problem and
solution.

( ) Circle the problem.

___ Underline
the solution.

The Tired Clock

▶ **Answer each question. Use the story and picture.**

1   Why did the clock thank Sara?

     ○ A. She turned off the alarm.

     ○ B. She changed its batteries.

     ○ C. She loved the clock.

     What helped you answer? _____

     _____

     _____

2   Which does NOT happen in real life?

     ○ A. Clocks speak.

     ○ B. Batteries run down.

     ○ C. Kids can solve problems.

     What helped you answer? _____

     _____

     _____

3   How does the picture fit the story?

     _____

     _____

     _____

     _____

     _____

Literary Passages: Close Reading (Grade 1)
© 2016 Scholastic Inc.

Name _____ Date _____

Pip Solves a Problem

Read the adventure story.
Then follow the directions in the box.

Pip the mouse had a problem.

She was stuck inside a car!

But Pip was a smart mouse.

She came up with a **clever** idea.

Pip climbed onto the steering wheel.

She jumped up and down on the horn.

BEEP! BEEP! BEEP!

Mr. Ling heard the noise.

What was wrong with his car?

He ran to it and opened the door.

Pip jumped out. She was free!

Text Marking

Find the problem and the solution.

☐ Draw boxes around the signal words **problem** and **idea**.

◯ Circle the problem.

___ Underline the solution.

Literary Passages: Close Reading (Grade 1)
© 2016 Scholastic Inc.

Name _____ Date _____

Pip Solves a Problem

▶ **Answer each question. Use the story and picture.**

1 Which word means the same as **clever**?

○ A. stuck   ○ B. smart   ○ C. free

What helped you answer? _____

_____

_____

2 Who is Mr. Ling?

○ A. a mouse   ○ B. a runner   ○ C. a car owner

What helped you answer? _____

_____

_____

3 Explain why Pip jumped on the horn.

_____

_____

_____

_____

_____

_____

Name _____ Date _____

Puppy School

Read the dog story.

Then follow the directions in the box.

Ramón got a puppy named Viva.

She barks a lot.

She barks to go outside.

She barks for treats and playtime.

Ramón has a problem.

How can he tell when she is barking

to go out?

Ramón thought of two answers.

One is to teach Viva to **fetch** her leash.

The other is to hang bells from a doorknob.

He can teach her to ring them to go out.

Puppy school starts today!

★ **Text Marking** ★

Find the problem and
the solutions.

☐ Draw boxes around
the signal words
problem and
answers.

⬭ Circle the problem.

___ Underline
two solutions.

Name _____ Date _____

Puppy School

▶ **Answer each question. Use the story and picture.**

1 Which word means the same as **fetch**?

　○ A. bring　　　○ B. ring　　　○ C. fix

What helped you answer? _____

_____

_____

2 What is Ramón's problem with Viva?

　○ A. Viva chews up shoes.

　○ B. Viva barks a lot.

　○ C. Ramón cannot tell what Viva wants when she barks.

What helped you answer? _____

_____

_____

3 What does the last sentence mean?

_____

_____

_____

_____

_____

_____

Literary Passages: Close Reading (Grade 1)
© 2016 Scholastic Inc.

Two Small Pets

Read the pet story.

Then follow the directions in the box.

Lulu has two pets.

One pet is a finch.

A finch is a bird.

Lulu calls him Feather.

The other pet is a crab.

Lulu calls her Shelly.

Shelly is very shy.

Both pets live in cages.

Lulu feeds them every day.

★ **Text Marking** ★

Compare Feather and Shelly.

☐ Draw a box around
the signal word **both**.

⬭ Circle one way the pets are alike.

Name _____ Date _____

Two Small Pets

▶ **Answer each question. Use the story and picture.**

1 Who is Shelly?

○ A. a child   ○ B. a crab   ○ C. a finch

What helped you answer? _____

_____

_____

2 What is a way that Feather and Shelly are ALIKE?

○ A. They eat the same things.

○ B. Both have shells.

○ C. Both are Lulu's pets.

What helped you answer? _____

_____

_____

3 Describe one way that Feather and Shelly are DIFFERENT.

_____

_____

_____

_____

_____

Literary Passages: Close Reading (Grade 1)
© 2016 Scholastic Inc.

Name _____ Date _____

Safe Trails

Read the nature story.

Then follow the directions in the box.

Ranger Roz works in a big park.

Her job is to check the trails.

She keeps them safe and clear.

Yesterday she hiked the long Rim Trail.

It is mostly flat and smooth.

It has gently rolling hills in places.

Today she is hiking up the high Peak Trail.

It is unlike the Rim Trail.

It goes up a mountain.

It is steep and rocky.

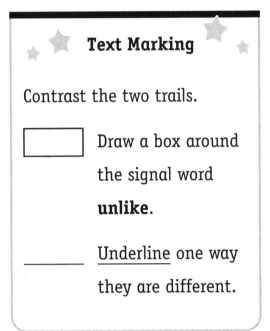

★ **Text Marking**

Contrast the two trails.

Draw a box around the signal word **unlike**.

_____ Underline one way they are different.

Literary Passages: Close Reading (Grade 1)
© 2016 Scholastic Inc.

Name _____ Date _____

Safe Trails

▶ **Answer each question. Use the story and picture.**

1 How are Rim Trail and Peak Trail ALIKE?

○ A. Both are steep.

○ B. Both are smooth.

○ C. Both are in a big park.

What helped you answer? _____

_____

_____

2 What is Ranger Roz's job?

○ A. She checks the trails for safety.

○ B. She teaches people how to hike.

○ C. She makes maps of the park.

What helped you answer? _____

_____

_____

3 Think about the two trails. Look at the picture.
Which trail would be harder to hike? Explain.

_____

_____

_____

_____

Literary Passages: Close Reading (Grade 1)
© 2016 Scholastic Inc.

Name _____ Date _____

Fox and Cat

Read the fable.

Then follow the directions in the box.

Fox and Cat lived in Woody Forest.

Both had tricks to stay safe.

Cat had only one trick.

But Fox had a whole bag of them.

Fox felt sorry for Cat.

Then along came a hunter.

Cat used her trick—she raced

up a tree to hide.

Fox opened his bag of tricks.

Which one should he use?

He could not decide.

So the hunter grabbed poor Fox.

All his tricks went to waste.

★ Text Marking ★

Compare and contrast
Fox and Cat.

☐ Draw boxes around
the signal words:
both and **but**

⬭ Circle one way
they are alike.

____ Underline one way
they are different.

Literary Passages: Close Reading (Grade 1)
© 2016 Scholastic Inc.

Name _____   Date _____

Fox and Cat

▶ **Answer each question. Use the fable and picture.**

1 Why did Fox feel sorry for Cat?

  ○ A. Cat was afraid of hunters.

  ○ B. Cat didn't have a bushy tail.

  ○ C. Cat had only one trick to stay safe.

What helped you answer? _____

_____

_____

2 What was Cat's trick?

  ○ A. hiding in a tree

  ○ B. scratching the hunter

  ○ C. pretending to be dead

What helped you answer? _____

_____

_____

3 Fox had a whole bag of tricks to stay safe. So why did Fox get caught?

_____

_____

_____

_____

Literary Passages: Close Reading (Grade 1)
© 2016 Scholastic Inc.

Cartoon Characters

Read the descriptions.

Then follow the directions in the box.

Bowtie Bunny and Patrol Pup

are both cartoon animals.

They are alike in one other way.

Both star in their own TV shows.

Bowtie Bunny and Patrol Pup

are different, too.

Bowtie Bunny is calm and clever.

She does magic tricks.

She can disappear inside a hat.

But Patrol Pup is jumpy.

He is not very smart.

He jumps at everyone.

He jumps at everything.

He even jumps at his own shadow!

Text Marking

Compare and contrast
the two cartoon animals.

☐ Draw boxes around
the signal words
both, **alike**,
different, and **but**.

⬭ Circle two ways
they are alike.

___ Underline two ways
they are different.

Name _____ Date _____

Cartoon Characters

▶ **Answer each question. Use the descriptions and picture.**

1 Which is TRUE about Patrol Pup?

○ A. He does magic tricks.

○ B. He wears a bowtie.

○ C. He jumps a lot.

What helped you answer? _____

_____

_____

2 How are Bowtie Bunny and Patrol Pup ALIKE?

○ A. Both are calm.

○ B. Both are on TV shows.

○ C. Both are real animals.

What helped you answer? _____

_____

_____

3 How can you tell that Patrol Pup is not very smart?

_____

_____

_____

_____

Literary Passages: Close Reading (Grade 1)

Answer Key

Sample Text Markings

Passage 1: Coach Sam

1. C; Sample answer: I picked C because it says so in the fourth sentence.

2. A; Sample answer: It says in the second sentence that he knows the game well.

3. Sample answer: Sam has played soccer since he was four, so he has played for many years.

Sample Text Markings

Passage 2: Kitchen Brothers

1. A; Sample answer: I picked A because it says so in the first sentence of the story.

2. C; Sample answer: I picked a meal of something each brother would make— a soup and a bread.

3. Sample answer: Juan is the one on the left. He is making bread.

Page 14 worksheet

Coach Sam

Read the sports story.
Then follow the directions in the box.

(Sam) has played soccer
since he was four.
He knows the game well.
Now Sam is 44.
He coaches a soccer team.
All the players are in first grade.
Sam helps them kick better.
He shows them how to stop a ball
with their feet.
Sam is a good coach.
He makes soccer fun.

Text Marking

Think about the story.

⬭ Circle WHO the story is about.

____ Underline one detail about that person.

14

Literary Passages: Close Reading (Grade 1)
© 2016 Scholastic Inc.

Page 16 worksheet

Kitchen Brothers

Read the cooking story.
Then follow the directions in the box.

(Juan) and (Rico) are brothers.
Both are good cooks.
Juan bakes breads.
He works the dough.
He knows just when it is ready.
He makes each bread into a shape.
His best is star bread with nuts.
Rico makes soups and stews.
He loves mixing flavors.
His best dish is lamb and rice stew.
He tastes as he cooks.
It is just right! YUM!

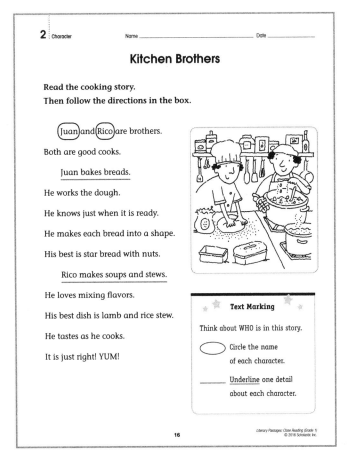

Text Marking

Think about WHO is in this story.

⬭ Circle the name of each character.

____ Underline one detail about each character.

16

Literary Passages: Close Reading (Grade 1)
© 2016 Scholastic Inc.

54

Getting Across

Read the folktale.
Then follow the directions in the box.

A hungry (goat) spotted a green field

that looked tasty. But it was across a river.

She stepped onto a wooden bridge.

"STOP!" yelled the mean (troll)

who lived below it. "You cannot cross MY bridge!"

"Please, I am hungry," said the goat politely.

"I only want to get to that green field."

"NO!" roared the angry troll.

"Okay, then, I will swim across."

And she bravely did just that.

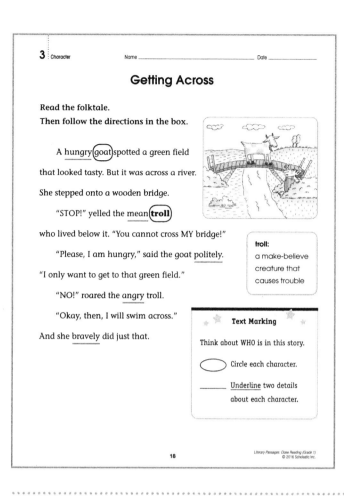

troll:
a make-believe creature that causes trouble

> ⭐ **Text Marking** ⭐
>
> Think about WHO is in this story.
>
> ⬭ Circle each character.
>
> ___ Underline two details about each character.

◀ Sample Text Markings

Passage 3: Getting Across

1. B; Sample answer: I picked B because it says so two times in the story.

2. C; Sample answer: It says this when the troll yells "STOP!"

3. Sample answer: It's probably easier just to walk across a bridge than to swim across a river.

The Legend of Swampy Pond

Read the legend.
Then follow the directions in the box.

Do you know about (Swampy Pond?)

The pond looks dark and deep.

The water feels cool.

On a hot summer day, it might seem

just right for a swim.

But old folks tell scary stories about it.

They say a giant catfish lives in that pond.

Nobody has ever seen it.

Nobody wants to.

> ⭐ **Text Marking** ⭐
>
> Think about the legend.
>
> ⬭ Circle WHERE the legend takes place.
>
> ___ Underline one detail about this place.

◀ Sample Text Markings

Passage 4: The Legend of Swampy Pond

1. B; Sample answer: I picked B because that's what the old folks say makes it a scary place.

2. A; Sample answer: I picked A because the second sentence in the legend says this.

3. Sample answer: It looks a little like it has whiskers, like a cat has.

Passage 5: Never Mind, March

1. C; Sample answer: I picked C because March is trying to blow the winter away to get ready for April and May—that's spring.

2. B; Sample answer: I picked B because the poem is about March winds blowing.

3. Sample answer: It shows the March wind as a cloud with a face, blowing hard with its mouth.

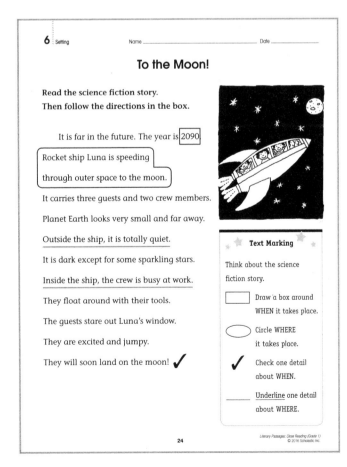

Passage 6: To the Moon!

1. C; Sample answer: I picked C because the year 2090 is many years away from now.

2. A; Sample answer: I picked A because it says this in the middle of the story.

3. Sample answer: I think the spaceship will land on the moon, and the guests and crew will get to walk on it.

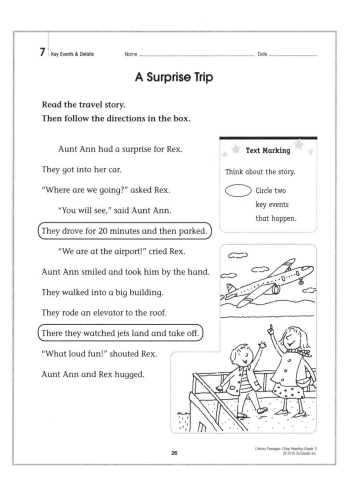

Passage 7: A Surprise Trip

1. B; Sample answer: I picked B because that's what the story is about.

2. C; Sample answer: I picked C because they were watching jets land and take off, and jets are noisy. The story says nothing about music or crowds.

3. Sample answer: I think she knew Rex was about to have a great time.

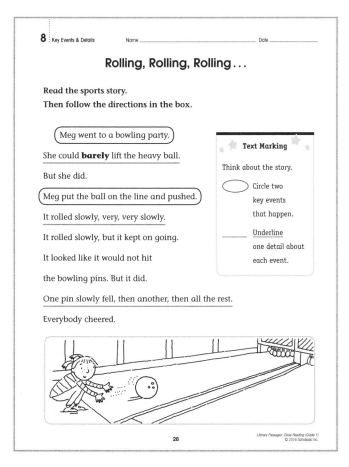

Passage 8: Rolling, Rolling, Rolling...

1. C; Sample answer: I picked C because the ball was heavy, and that would make it hard to pick up. *Barely* and *hardly* both mean about the same thing.

2. A; Sample answer: I picked A because that's just what happened. All the pins fell down.

3. Sample answer: I see how big the ball is for a kid. I can tell that Meg had to push it to get it to roll. So she could only make it roll slowly.

Literary Passages: Close Reading (Grade 1)
© 2016 Scholastic Inc.

Go Fly a Kite!

Read the springtime story.
Then follow the directions in the box.

Ko went to the park to fly his kite.

Many people had the same idea

on that windy spring day.

Soon Ko's kite was high in the sky.

Suddenly, his kite got tangled

with another one.

They came crashing down together.

Ko raced to his kite.

A girl raced to her kite.

But when they got there,

both children smiled.

Ko's kite looked like a butterfly.

And so did hers.

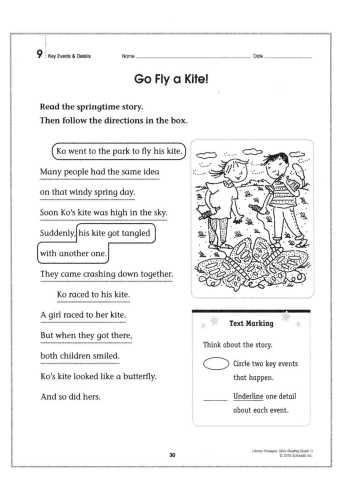

Text Marking

Think about the story.

◯ Circle two key events that happen.

___ Underline one detail about each event.

Literary Passages: Close Reading (Grade 1)
© 2016 Scholastic Inc.

◀ Sample Text Markings

Passage 9: Go Fly a Kite!

1. B; Sample answer: I picked B because the story said it was a windy day, and that's all I know for sure.

2. A; Sample answer: I picked A because that's what the story said.

3. Sample answer: They smiled because they both had the same kind of kite.

In the Attic

Read the mystery story.
Then follow the directions in the box.

Taye climbed to the dusty attic,

which was full of old boxes and junk.

He opened a wooden trunk.

Inside he found a furry wolf mask.

Taye put it on and acted wild.

Suddenly, he howled in surprise.

Another wolf was in the attic,

staring at him!

Taye raced downstairs to his room

and shut the door.

When he looked in his mirror,

he smiled. What did he see?

Text Marking

Think about the story.

◯ Circle two key events that happen.

___ Underline two details about each event.

Literary Passages: Close Reading (Grade 1)
© 2016 Scholastic Inc.

◀ Sample Text Markings

Passage 10: In the Attic

1. C; Sample answer: I picked C because the story said he found a furry wolf mask.

2. A; Sample answer: I picked A because I think that's what happened when he thought he saw another wolf.

3. Sample answer: I think he saw himself in the wolf mask and smiled because the wolf he ran away from was himself in a mirror that was in the attic.

Literary Passages: Close Reading (Grade 1)
© 2016 Scholastic Inc.

A Silly Dream

Read the fantasy story.
Then follow the directions in the box.

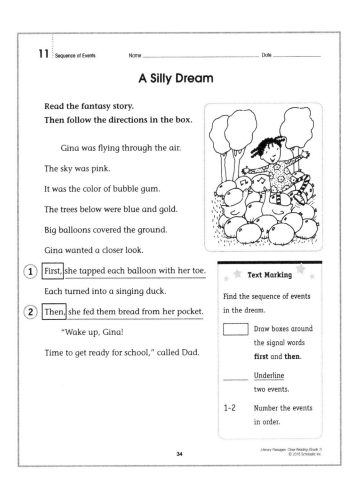

Gina was flying through the air.

The sky was pink.

It was the color of bubble gum.

The trees below were blue and gold.

Big balloons covered the ground.

Gina wanted a closer look.

(1) First, she tapped each balloon with her toe.

Each turned into a singing duck.

(2) Then, she fed them bread from her pocket.

"Wake up, Gina!

Time to get ready for school," called Dad.

★ ★ Text Marking ★ ★

Find the sequence of events
in the dream.

☐ Draw boxes around
the signal words
first and **then**.

___ Underline
two events.

1-2   Number the events
in order.

34

Literary Passages: Close Reading (Grade 1)
© 2016 Scholastic Inc.

◀ Sample Text Markings

Passage 11: A Silly Dream

1. A; Sample answer: I picked A because I read this in the third sentence.

2. C; Sample answer: I picked C because it said that in the story.

3. Sample answer: I think it was a dream because kids can't really fly, ducks can't sing, and her dad woke her up at the end. Also, the title is "A Silly Dream."

Treasure Hunt

Read the birthday story.
Then follow the directions in the box.

It was Nick's birthday.

He was going on a treasure hunt.

He had a list of what to look for.

Things were hidden all over his home.

(1) First, he found the kazoo.

It was hiding inside Mom's fuzzy slipper.

(2) Next, he found the comic book.

It was tucked under the green pillow.

(3) Then, he found the set of star stickers.

They were behind the big salad bowl.

Nick had five more birthday treasures

to find. Where might they be?

★ ★ Text Marking ★ ★

Mark the sequence
of treasures Nick found.

☐ Draw boxes around
the signal words
first, **next**,
and **then**.

___ Underline three
things Nick found.

1-2-3   Number the treasures
in order.

36

Literary Passages: Close Reading (Grade 1)
© 2016 Scholastic Inc.

◀ Sample Text Markings

Passage 12: Treasure Hunt

1. C; Sample answer: I picked C because I read the order of the things he found, and the comic book was second.

2. B; Sample answer: I picked B because it said that in the story.

3. Sample answer: I think Nick will keep looking for the other things on the list until he finds them all.

Painting Puff

Read the art story.
Then follow the directions in the box.

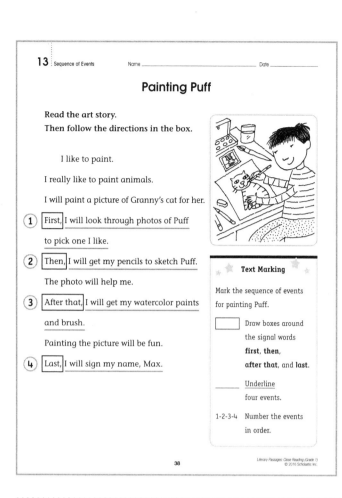

I like to paint.

I really like to paint animals.

I will paint a picture of Granny's cat for her.

(1) First, I will look through photos of Puff

to pick one I like.

(2) Then, I will get my pencils to sketch Puff.

The photo will help me.

(3) After that, I will get my watercolor paints

and brush.

Painting the picture will be fun.

(4) Last, I will sign my name, Max.

★☆ ★   **Text Marking**   ★ ☆

Mark the sequence of events
for painting Puff.

☐ Draw boxes around
the signal words
first, **then**,
after that, and **last**.

___ Underline
four events.

1-2-3-4 Number the events
in order.

Literary Passages: Close Reading (Grade 1)
© 2016 Scholastic Inc.

38

◀ Sample Text Markings

Passage 13: Painting Puff

1. A; Sample answer: I picked A because the person telling the story says he will sign his name, *Max*.

2. B; Sample answer: I picked B because it said that in the story.

3. Sample answer: I think a cat wouldn't sit still long enough.

The Tired Clock

Read the fantasy story.
Then follow the directions in the box.

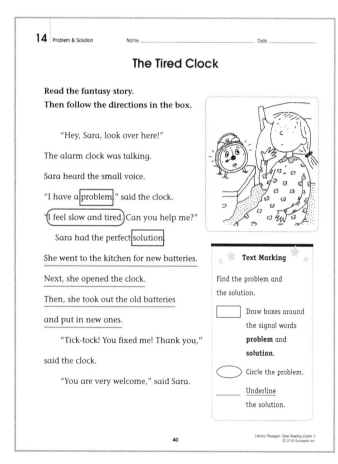

"Hey, Sara, look over here!"

The alarm clock was talking.

Sara heard the small voice.

"I have a problem," said the clock.

"I feel slow and tired. Can you help me?"

Sara had the perfect solution.

She went to the kitchen for new batteries.

Next, she opened the clock.

Then, she took out the old batteries

and put in new ones.

"Tick-tock! You fixed me! Thank you,"

said the clock.

"You are very welcome," said Sara.

★☆ ★   **Text Marking**   ★ ☆

Find the problem and
the solution.

☐ Draw boxes around
the signal words
problem and
solution.

◯ Circle the problem.

___ Underline
the solution.

Literary Passages: Close Reading (Grade 1)
© 2016 Scholastic Inc.

40

◀ Sample Text Markings

Passage 14: The Tired Clock

1. B; Sample answer: I picked B because the story says Sara put new batteries in, and the clock felt better.

2. A; Sample answer: I picked A because B and C happen in real life, but clocks can't really speak.

3. Sample answer: The clock in the picture looks tired and droopy, like the talking clock. And it has a mouth for talking.

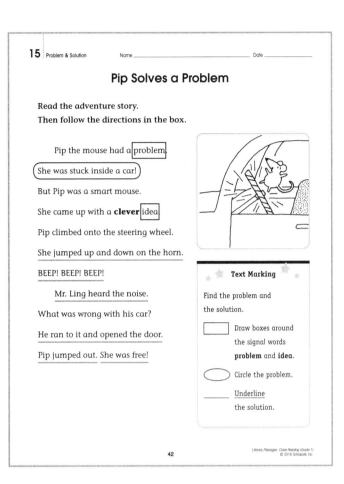

◄ Sample Text Markings

Passage 15: Pip Solves a Problem

1. B; Sample answer: I picked B because the story says that Pip was smart and came up with a good idea. Also, A and C don't make sense.

2. C; Sample answer: I picked C because the story says he ran to his car.

3. Sample answer: Pip jumped on the horn to make noise. That made Mr. Ling come to the car and open the door.

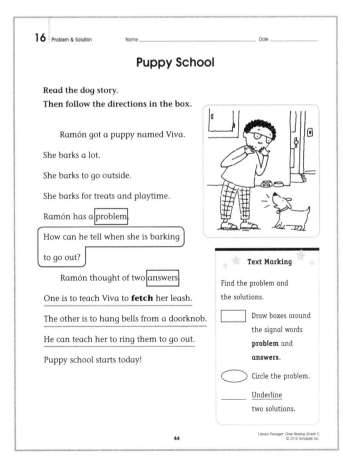

◄ Sample Text Markings

Passage 16: Puppy School

1. A; Sample answer: I picked A because it makes the most sense. Ramón needs to put Viva on her leash to go out, so he wants to teach her to bring him her leash.

2. C; Sample answer: I picked C because the story says that he cannot tell when Viva needs to go out.

3. Sample answer: I think it means that Ramón will start teaching Viva right away to fetch her leash and ring the bells.

Literary Passages: Close Reading (Grade 1)
© 2016 Scholastic Inc.

Sample Text Markings

Two Small Pets

17 Compare & Contrast   Name _____ Date _____

Read the pet story.
Then follow the directions in the box.

Lulu has two pets.

One pet is a finch.

A finch is a bird.

Lulu calls him Feather.

The other pet is a crab.

Lulu calls her Shelly.

Shelly is very shy.

Both pets live in cages.

Lulu feeds them every day.

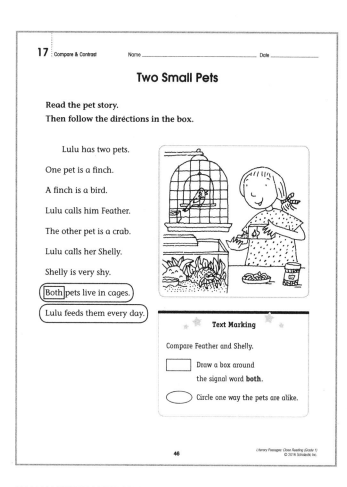

Text Marking

Compare Feather and Shelly.

☐ Draw a box around the signal word **both**.

⬭ Circle one way the pets are alike.

46

Passage 17: Two Small Pets

1. B; Sample answer: I picked B because it says that Lulu calls her crab Shelly.

2. C; Sample answer: I picked C because the first sentence says that Lulu has two pets. Both Feather and Shelly are her pets. Also, Feather is a bird and would not have a shell. And the story does not tell about what they eat.

3. Sample answer: They are different kinds of animals. Feather is a bird, but Shelly is a crab.

Safe Trails

18 Compare & Contrast   Name _____ Date _____

Read the nature story.
Then follow the directions in the box.

Ranger Roz works in a big park.

Her job is to check the trails.

She keeps them safe and clear.

Yesterday she hiked the long Rim Trail.

It is mostly flat and smooth.

It has gently rolling hills in places.

Today she is hiking up the high Peak Trail.

It is unlike the Rim Trail.

It goes up a mountain.

It is steep and rocky.

Text Marking

Contrast the two trails.

☐ Draw a box around the signal word **unlike**.

___ Underline one way they are different.

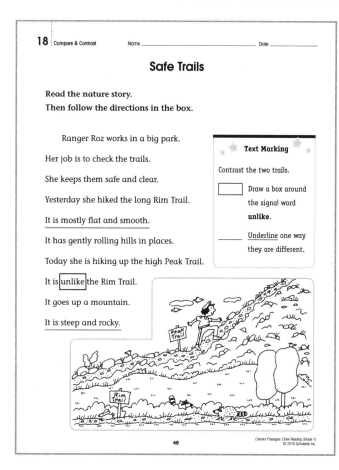

48

Passage 18: Safe Trails

1. C; Sample answer: I picked C because it says this at the very beginning. Plus, A and B are not ways that both trails are alike.

2. A; Sample answer: I picked A because the story tells that she checks the trails for safety in the second and third sentences.

3. Sample answer: I think Peak Trail would be harder because it goes up a mountain and is steep and rocky.

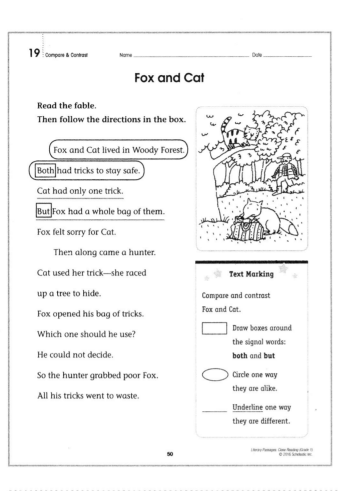

Sample Text Markings

Passage 19: Fox and Cat

1. C; Sample answer: I picked C because it says this in the third sentence.

2. A; Sample answer: I picked A because the story said that is what Cat did.

3. Sample answer: Fox could not decide which trick to use. So, while he was deciding, the hunter grabbed him.

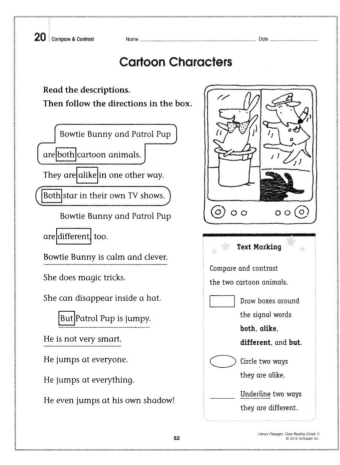

Sample Text Markings

Passage 20: Cartoon Characters

1. C; Sample answer: I picked C because the story says he jumps at everyone and everything.

2. B; Sample answer: I picked B because A and C are not true for both.

3. Sample answer: I think he is not smart if he jumps at his own shadow.

Literary Passages: Close Reading (Grade 1)
© 2016 Scholastic Inc.

Notes